FRUIT OF THE SPIRIT

SELF-CONTROL

Fruit of the Spirit Study Guide Series

Love

Joy

Peace

Patience

Kindness

Goodness

Faithfulness

Gentleness

Self-Control

CALVIN MILLER

FRUIT OF THE SPIRIT

SELF-CONTROL

Published in Nashville, Tennessee, by Thomas Nelson. Thomas Nelson is a trademark of Thomas Nelson, Inc.

Typesetting by Gregory C. Benoit Publishing, Old Mystic, CT

Thomas Nelson, Inc., titles may be purchased in bulk for educational, business, fund-raising, or sales promotional use. For information, please e-mail SpecialMarkets@ThomasNelson.com.

ISBN: 978-1-4185-2844-7

Printed in the United States of America
08 09 10 11 12 RRD 9 8 7 6 5 4 3 2 1

TABLE OF CONTENTS

But the fruit of the Spirit is love, joy, peace, patience, kindness, goodness, faithfulness, gentleness and self-control. Against such things there is no law.

—Galatians 5:22–23

INTRODUCTION

The Bible teaches that self-control is a characteristic that accompanies the other fruits of the Spirit. When we allow God total control of our lives, we gain his ability to say no to selfish desires and self-destructive behavior.

Self-control demands that we evaluate the possible consequences of our actions before we decide to do something, not after the fact. We can pause right here and have a moment of confession—we've all done things we wished we hadn't done. Some of us still live with the consequences. The alcoholic regrets his first drink. The emphysema sufferer regrets her first cigarette. The pregnant teen regrets her lack of self-control. The list goes on and on.

God doesn't want us to live regretting the past, so he empowers us to overcome the desires we face. This is the self-control he brings into our lives as a part of our salvation experience. We can choose to live his way, or we can go it alone.

Many believers attempt to go it alone because they believe they can handle the temptation. Willpower, however, is no match for some of today's personal threats. The avenues of life are littered with the broken lives of people who have made bad decisions because they refused to let God's presence overcome their weaknesses.

Paul listed self-control as one of the fruits of the Spirit because he knew that a believer without self-control would be an easy target for Satan's schemes. Satan's desire is to destroy believers and the reputations of those who claim to know God. In our time, we have seen many professing believers discredited because of their lack of self-control.

God's reputation is at stake in the way we live. When we let him down, we tell the world that our desires are more important than his expectations. In effect, we look God in the face and say, "You're not as important as me." Few people would confess to making that statement to God. Yet many make that statement in the way they live their lives.

In this study, we'll be reintroduced to the biblical concept of self-control. We'll see how it can change the way we live and the way we represent God. We'll discover how it can influence where we go, how we talk, what we watch, and how we spend God's money. How you live tells the world what you really think of God. When we live with self-control, we show the world that true fulfillment can be found apart from the world's ways. Self-control is the pathway to the abundant life ... and that's the life worth living!

HOW TO USE THIS GUIDE

Galatians 5:22–23 is not a plan to achieve better faith. Rather, it is a description of God's personal gifts to all of us. If we follow God and seek his blessing, then the fruits of the Spirit are a natural overflow in our relationship with God. We are to grow in character so that one day we will reflect the image of our Lord.

This series of nine six-week studies will clearly focus your spiritual life to become more like Christ. Each study guide is divided into six weeks, and each of the six-week courses covers one of the fruits of the Spirit. Participants simply read each daily study and answer the questions at the end of each devotional. This prepares everyone for the group discussion at the end of the week.

Each week features a similar pattern that explores one aspect of that study's fruit of the Spirit. The first lesson establishes the aspect of the fruit to be explored throughout the week. The second lesson looks at the week's theme as it relates to God's purpose in the life of the believer. The third lesson looks at the week's theme as it relates to the believer's relationship with Christ. The fourth lesson explores how the fruit is relevant in service to others. And in the fifth lesson, the theme is related to personal worship. A sixth lesson is included as a bonus study, and focuses on either a biblical character who modeled this particular fruit, or a key parable that brings the theme into focus.

Each weeklong study should conclude in a group review. The weekly group discussion serves as a place to understand the practical side of the theme and receive encouragement and feedback on the journey to become more Christlike. For the study to have the character-transforming effect God desires, it is important for the participant to spend ten to twenty minutes a day reading the Scripture passage and the devotional, and to think through the two questions for the day. If each participant reads all of the questions beforehand, it greatly enhances the group dynamic. Each participant should choose three or four questions to discuss during the group session.

These simple guidelines will help make group time productive. Take a total of about forty-five minutes to answer and discuss the questions. Each person need not answer every question, but be sure all members participate. You can stimulate participation by having everyone respond to an icebreaker question. Have each group member answer the first of the six questions listed at the end of the week, and leave the remaining questions open-ended. Or, make up your own icebreaker question, such as: What color best represents the day you are having? What is your favorite movie? Or, how old were you when you had your first kiss?

No one should respond to all of the questions. Keep in mind that if you are always talking, the others are not. It is essential that everyone contribute. If you notice that someone is not participating, ask that group member which question is the most relevant. Be sensitive if something is keeping that member from contributing. Don't ask someone to read or pray aloud unless you know that the member is comfortable with such a task.

Always start and end your time with prayer. Sometimes it helps to have each person say what he or she plans to do with the lesson that week. Remember to reserve ten minutes for group prayer. You might want to keep a list of requests and answers to prayer at the back of this book.

Week 1: Self-Control—Part of Coming to Maturity

Memory Passage for the Week: Philippians 2:12–13

Day 1: Self-Control—Part of Coming to Maturity
Self-control is the instrument God gives us to plot our path to maturity in Christ. 2 Samuel 11:1–5

Day 2: The Purpose of God in My Life
Loving God will result in sexual purity. Sexual purity makes us the kind of vessel God can use. Proverbs 5:15–20.

Day 3: My Relationship with Christ
The refining work of God cleanses us until our impurities are gone and we move into a more Christlike holiness. Job 23:10.

Day 4: My Service to Others
Jesus remarked that only those who produce the most rigorous spiritual disciplines can ever war effectively against Satan. Mark 9:14–17, 29.

Day 5: My Personal Worship
Nothing is sweeter than worship when we meet God having been cleansed of all sin and when our desire for secret sins has been cleansed as well. Psalm 51:1–12.

Day 6: A Character Study on Jacob
Genesis 27:1–29; 29:15–30; 30:25–32; 31:17–21

Day 7: Group Discussion

Day 1: Self-Control—Part of Coming to Maturity
Read 2 Samuel 11:1–5

"In the spring, at the time when kings go off to war" (2 Samuel 11:1) was the "once-upon-a-time" with which Samuel began his tale of David's affair with Bathsheba. Why are the words "at the time when kings go off to war" so significant? Because this was probably the first time in his life when David—unlike other kings—did not go off to war.

In this short phrase it is clear that David sent his army into the field without him. He chose to leave the rigors of military life and infantry for a life of ease. While his soldiers were suffering through the inclemency of war, David wasn't suffering at all. In other words, David, who had always opted for a life of self-denial, began to opt for a life of self-indulgence.

"Taking a load off" is how our comfort-loving society would phrase it. But taking a load off led to other indulgences. The king allowed himself all the comforts his castle had to offer. And with no regard for morality, he watched one of his soldier's wives take a bath. Uriah was the soldier's name. He was a Hittite and a mercenary, one of David's best friends, but a Gentile who was easily dispensed with. Uriah—unlike David—was denying himself the comforts of home life while he risked his life to expand David's empire.

Watching Bathsheba led David to lusting, and lusting to adultery. The adultery finally resulted in a pregnancy, a murder, and a huge cover-up operation the king instituted in an attempt to hide his sin and protect his reputation. When indulgence comes into our lives, self-control leaves by the back door. In David's case, the great writer of many psalms became an indulgent adulterer and murderer.

Once we permit ourselves one sin and squelch our inner remorse, remorse loses its voice as we commit other sins. The only hope we have is to make self-control the keeper of our inner lives. Let us then ask God to make self-control the instrument he gives us to plot our path to maturity in Christ.

Questions for Personal Reflection

1. What are the areas in which self-control is a problem for you?

2. How can a renewed commitment to God help you in these areas?

Day 2: The Purpose of God in My Life
Read Proverbs 5:15–20

This metaphor on fidelity in marriage is one of the most powerful in the Scriptures. The metaphor pushes the idea that in every marriage, sexual fidelity is the hallmark of God's blessing.

Yet in every age the temptation to be unfaithful endures. Sexual self-control always results in keeping our hearts free from infidelity. "To drink water from our own cistern" means we have agreed with God that we are willing to practice sexual self-control, and that any suggestion of sexual infidelity injures not just our relationship with God but with our fellow human beings as well.

Indeed we cannot live out God's purpose for our lives while we indulge in immorality. God requires a clean vessel into which he can pour his purposes. No doubt this notion will seem quaint and old-fashioned to our culture. The question that regulates our "new morality" in this area relates to, "who gets hurt" more than "what God said." First, "who gets hurt?" If the answer is nobody, then "those who seek to indulge are free to do it." Second, "does it feel good?" If it does, then "why deny the joy?"

In a recent survey, 12 percent of ministers—in total confidence—said they had committed sexual indiscretions for which they "had never been caught." While they had apparently "gotten away with their sin," none of them felt that their indulgence had enabled them to serve God with a pure heart. Self-control alone will make that happen.

Self-control gives God a voice in our sexual ethics. Without this voice, the world would be depraved and incapable of holiness.

Questions for Personal Reflection

1. What is your plan of escape when faced with temptation to violate God's moral principles?

2. What are your sexual standards, and how do they compare to God's standards? What should you change about your standards?

Day 3: My Relationship with Christ
Read Job 23:10

Holiness is the only soil in which a relationship with Christ can be root-
ed. But how hard do we strive to arrive at holiness? Do we simply decide
"to be holy" and then try to be good enough to be welcomed into God's
circle of friends?

Job said that God tests us before we "come forth as gold" (Job 23:10).
Trials do indeed refine us as if in a refiner's fire. One can imagine a clump
of gold ore protesting the foundry. The metallurgist may seem cruel as
he heats the gold beyond endurance. But as gold becomes smelted in the
pain and the flame, it is purified into true worth.

Yet who is so mature that he welcomes the refining fire? Almost no
one. The discipline of God hurts. Hebrews reminds us that God's discipline is on our behalf.

> *"My son, do not make light of the Lord's discipline,*
> *and do not lose heart when he rebukes you,*
> *because the Lord disciplines those he loves,*
> *and he punishes everyone he accepts as a son."*
> *Endure hardship as discipline; God is treating you*
> *as sons. For what son is not disciplined by his father? If you*
> *are not disciplined (and everyone undergoes discipline), then*
> *you are illegitimate children and not true sons.... God disciplines*

us for our good, that we may share in his holiness. No
discipline seems pleasant at the time, but painful. Later on,
however, it produces a harvest of righteousness and peace
for those who have been trained by it.
—Hebrews 12:5–11

Almost every time we meet a great believer whose life is schooled in holiness, that believer has passed through the furnaces of God. Those souls have wept, and their tears have purified their worldviews, their value systems, and their hearts.

Then tried and cleansed, they moved freely into the presence of God. They knew at last the truth of 1 Peter 1:16—"Be holy, for I am holy" (NKJV). Then they were at home in the presence and fellowship of God, for they had become more like him than they ever dreamed possible.

Questions for Personal Reflection

1. In what ways is God molding you into his likeness?

2. What have been the end results of God's discipline in your life?

Day 4: My Service to Others

Read Mark 9:14-17, 29

The disciples in this passage were hoping to climb the spiritual equivalent of Mt. Everest after only practicing their spiritual disciplines on an anthill. Jesus told them that some feats could only be achieved by those who condition themselves to be saints of self-denial.

We are not told if the disciples were annoyed that their easy-come-easy-go spirituality wouldn't hold up very well when they were face to face with Satan. But their frail spirituality should speak clearly to us, that the greatest achievements of even the best saints were always the outgrowth of utter discipline.

What are the requirements that make for utter discipline? Paul rehearsed the rigors of such discipleship with Timothy:

> *You then, my son, be strong in the grace that is in Christ Jesus.... Endure hardship with us like a good soldier of Christ Jesus. No one serving as a soldier gets involved in civilian affairs—he wants to please his commanding officer. Similarly, if anyone competes as an athlete, he does not receive the victor's crown unless he competes according to the rules.*
> —2 Timothy 2:1–5

Those who want to achieve great things for God need to practice the great disciplines of spirituality. Jesus said prayer and fasting are the real evidences of a robust inner faith. Self-control is the first step of spiritual discipline. Those who cannot control their appetites and who frame all of life in their indulgences can hardly be expected to enter into successful spiritual combat that tries the souls even of saints.

Questions for Personal Reflection

1. In what ways are you pursuing spiritual strength?

2. Plot your spiritual growth over the past few months. Are you growing or treading water? How can you grow over the months to come?

Day 5: My Personal Worship
Read Psalm 51:1–12

This psalm is an exposé of the heart. Not only was it written by a person who was desirous of forgiveness, but it was the heart cry of a man hungry for a new lifestyle.

How very infrequently do those two issues come together? Most people want to be forgiven, but their plea for forgiveness leaves them without the slightest desire to truly become better people. Even as they seek cleansing they plan how they shall get dirty the next time.

The holiness we discussed earlier really comes when the plea for forgiveness and the desire to live a cleansed life come together. Holiness has a preemptive sinlessness about it. Holiness is that "second step" of self-control that seeks first to be forgiven for sin, but then to stop doing it altogether.

In Psalm 51, David realized that his sin was never a private affair. "Against you, you only" (v. 4) are four words of personal reformation that lead us into holy living. We cannot desire even the pleasure of our sin, for we cannot live free of this principle: wickedness that might bring pleasure for a season is adultery to God.

Personal reformation requires that we live in open confession before God. God has a simple formula for forgiveness and cleansing. It is found in 1 John 1:9: "If we confess our sins, he is faithful and just and will forgive us our sins and purify us from all unrighteousness."

If we do this, writes John, we will "walk in the light, as he is in the light," then we will "have fellowship one with another" (v. 7). David had to learn, as do we, that we cannot sin without fracturing our whole world of relationships. David's unconfessed sin prevented him from having a meaningful conversation with anybody—least of all God.

Our time of worship should include a time of confession. Let our times of praising God's holiness also be a time to invite him into every part of our lives, especially those areas where we lack self-control, that we may be holy before him. We will be rejuvenated by this worship, and our self-control will be energized in its driving desire to bring pleasure to our heavenly Father.

Questions for Personal Reflection

1. Is your life one of open confession before God? If not, why? If so, how does your openness affect your daily walk with God?

2. How have your sins affected your relationships with other people and with God?

Day 6: Jacob—An Agenda for Achievement

Read Genesis 27:1–29; 29:15–30; 30:25–32; 31:17–21

Jacob is not the sort of person we can turn to in order to point out sterling character. From the time he was born he was named the Supplanter or Heel Grabber. Being born the second of a set of twins, Jacob came out of the womb trying to grab the heel of Esau and pull him back in so he could be the firstborn himself (Genesis 25:24–26). From that point on, Jacob led a rather devious life.

Still, it must be remembered that he was the father of the twelve tribes of Israel and therefore most seriously involved in Abraham's lineage—the center of God's plan to bless the whole world through the Abrahamic covenant.

Jacob must also be credited as a good businessman—at least good at achieving his goals—even if he was not as honest as we would like. There are four evidences that Jacob was a man of self-control, the kind of self-control that creates its own agenda for achievement.

First, he stole his brother's blessing (Genesis 27:1–29). Rebekah obviously favored Jacob over Esau, his twin, and decided to help Jacob convince Isaac that he was Esau, and thus steal the blessing. So Jacob contrived an elaborate plan to do just that and deceived his old, blind father in order to reach his goal.

Second, after Jacob had fled to Paddan Aram, he went to work for Laban, and worked for seven years to win the hand of Rachel in marriage. But his father-in-law was as devious as Jacob, and so Jacob awoke the morning after his wedding to find he had married Leah, the heavily-veiled sister of Rachel. So he worked another seven years to get the woman he had missed the first time around (Genesis 29:15–30).

Third, Jacob devised a stratagem to multiply his own flocks and herds at his father-in-law's expense (Genesis 30:25–32, 37–43). He had earlier asked for the mottled animals in Laban's herd to be his, and Laban agreed. Then Jacob found a way to swindle Laban out of the stronger animals, while Laban retained the weaker, sicklier animals. In this way Jacob "grew exceedingly prosperous and came to own large flocks, and maidservants and menservants, and camels and donkeys" (Genesis 30:43).

Finally, Jacob moved away while Laban had his back turned, and thus appropriated all he could at Laban's expense (Genesis 31:17–21).

Jacob was a schemer and most devious, and he knew how to press his ambitions in self-controlled ways to get what he wanted out of life. But self-control must be done for godly reasons, and in this Jacob failed. If we can see that our own dreams for achievement can be handed over to God, then, surely, through self-control and personal discipline, we can acheive what is far more meaningful in God's eyes.

Questions for Personal Reflection

1. What are the immediate, short-term, and long-term dangers of failing to

exercise self-control?

2. How are you being held accountable for exercising godly self-control?

Day 7: Group Discussion

The following questions should take about forty-five minutes to answer and discuss. Each member should answer the first question, leaving the remaining questions open-ended. Everyone need not answer, but be sure all members participate.

1. *What are some of the indulgences in our lives that have negative spiritual effects?*

2. *Why is it so difficult to maintain moral purity in our culture?*

3.   *What are some of the trials that have shaped your spiritual life? How can your experiences help others understand God better?*

4.   *What are the signs of a robust faith and how are you developing this kind of faith?*

5. *What is holiness and how is it realized in our lives?*

6. *What are the evidences of self-control that you see in other people's lives? How can you develop more self-control?*

SELF-CONTROL 25

Week 2: Self-Control—The Mark of Obedience

Memory Passage for the Week: 2 Peter 1:5–7

Day 1: Self-Control—The Mark of Obedience

Over-indulgence and disobedience must be cleansed from our lives. We must forgive others for their lack of self-control just as we forgive ourselves for our own disobedience. Daniel 1:8–17.

Day 2: The Purpose of God in My Life

Whatever we do should exalt God. If we have any activity that detracts from his love, we must pray for the self-control to stop it. 1 Corinthians 10:31.

Day 3: My Relationship with Christ

Moses said self-control was a recipe with three ingredients: loving God, walking in his ways, and keeping his laws. Deuteronomy 30:16.

Day 4: My Service to Others

It is Christlike to live our lives so as not to sin against anyone's conscience. 1 Corinthians 8:9–10.

Day 5: My Personal Worship

When we are conformed to Christ's image, we love his Father just like he did, and our worship soars. Romans 12:1–2.

Day 6: A Character Study on Moses

Exodus 15:22–27; Numbers 20:6–13

Day 7: Group Discussion

Day 1: Self-Control—The Mark of Obedience
Read Daniel 1:8–17

Most evangelicals I know see what they eat and drink as the last bastion of self-control. Many wouldn't drink even a little wine and confess to it. They feel that while it might have been alright for Paul and Timothy, it would weaken their own reputations in the church. Most do agree that playing cards is alright if done quietly without poker chips. Thus, in recent years the five big no-no's that used to be focused on (cards, dancing, movies, alcohol, and tobacco) have been narrowed down.

Gluttony, however, is a rare subject of spiritual discussion. It is the sin kept on reserve, a more legitimate indulgence. If you need a certificate of moral permission for a real whopper of an iniquity, you can pile up your plate at the Sunday school potluck, and the church will sign off on gluttony.

I have always been struck by the odd inconsistency of obese evangelists preaching against alcohol abuse. How wicked we become in excusing our own indulgences while excoriating others for theirs. Self-forgiveness sometimes forgives the preacher while it calls the audience to task. Nowhere is this truer than in how many believers handle gluttony.

This permissible gluttony is an odd allowance, since the Bible condemned it so often. Furthermore, Scripture defines fasting as a manner of self-control that enhances the prayer life and deepens the Christ life.

This passage in Daniel speaks to the spoiling of life and health by overindulgence. Daniel survived very well on lean meals and water.

But simply surviving was not Daniel's goal. He wanted to thrive spiritually. He wanted to be sure that permissive gluttony did not leave him a poor lover of God. It's a fair question for us as well.

Questions for Personal Reflection

1. Are you more concerned with surviving spiritually or thriving spiritually?

Explain your response.

2. What are some ways in which your expectations of others are different than your expectations of yourself?

Day 2: The Purpose of God in My Life
Read 1 Corinthians 10:31

Whatever you do, do all to the glory of God. This simple little statement is the most positive of all guides to self-control. We try to learn self-control by making ourselves a big list of dos and don'ts and then making ourselves miserable with all the things that we deny ourselves. This is not to play down self-denial, but it is better to focus on what we can enjoy in Christ, rather than the things we are trying to avoid.

What is the purpose of God in your life? As simply as it can be put, it is to glorify God. How do you glorify him? By posting a long list of rules and by judging yourself and others by how well you follow them? Never! You merely ask yourself at every juncture of the Christ life whether what you are about to do does indeed glorify God. If not, don't do it. Again the rule is, whatever you do, do all to the glory of God.

Simple? Yes. But will it work?

Let's take something as practical as dieting. Don't we all neurotically try to let the thinner us, trapped inside the thicker us, get out? I had a friend who was fifty pounds overweight all his life. He had tried liquid diets, solid diets, lettuce diets, and spinach diets. He stayed fifty pounds overweight, resolving after every Saturday night pizza party that next week, he'd really lose weight. What delivered him was that he wrote 1 Corinthians 10:31 on a little white card. Then before every meal he took the card out and set it by his plate. Self-control was his. Gluttony was gone. By focusing on God an immersing himself in the Word, self-control came naturally. He discovered that 1 Corinthians 10:31 worked so well that he didn't have to wait for heaven to get a little closer to having his glorified body.

Questions for Personal Reflection

1. What commitment do you keep making but not keeping?

2. How can God help you keep your commitments? How do your bad habits affect the degree to which other people believe the reality of your commitment to God?

Day 3: My Relationship with Christ

Read Deuteronomy 30:16

The self-control that bears the mark of obedience will always enhance our relationship with Christ. When self-control is carried out, we yield the rewards. Moses said to Israel that there were three important steps to self-control (listed in Deuteronomy 30:16):

1. We must love the Lord our God. Loving God more than any other single force in our lives will enable us to practice self-control.
2. We must walk in his ways. So often in Scripture our union with Christ is pictured as a journey, a walk. We walk along with God, who instructs us as we grow toward spiritual maturity. Walking with God will in every case enhance our relationship with Christ as it results in a life of self-control.
3. We must keep his decree and laws. His commandments define the parameters of our self-control.

The rewards of our self-control are also three:

1. We will live and prosper. This is not referring to the rewards we receive in eternity; it is God's promise that self-control will bring a better life in the present.

2. We will increase. Life generally gets bigger in every way for those who learn the art of obedience.

3. We will experience the full blessing of God. This is the richest reward of all. God's full blessing brings immeasurable joy and meaning.

All in all, our walk with Christ will be as victorious as we are submissive. Our closeness to him and our self-control always keep the same happy ratio.

Questions for Personal Reflection

1. If spiritual victory is connected to spiritual obedience, what does your life say about your degree of obedience to God?

2. In what areas of life do you need to become more obedient to God?

Day 4: My Service to Others
Read 1 Corinthians 8:9–10

Our liberty in Christ is immense. Yet we are to rein in the wide latitudes of our choices. If Jesus approves an appetite for our enjoyment, we are free in Christ to enjoy it, with one exception: If someone can accuse us of being superficial or worldly for doing it. Then for the sake of those whom our liberty would injure, Christ asks us to desist from that activity.

How are we to consider what is permitted by Christ versus what is not permitted by Christ because it wounds a weaker individual? I grew up in a religion that forbade shopping or eating in a public restaurant on the Lord's Day. So for years after I began pastoring my first church, I refused to go to a restaurant on Sunday. While other church members regularly ate out after worship services, our family did not. It was not that our family considered it to be wrong, but that there were a few in our congregation who considered it to be ungodly. So for their sake, we ate at home. We did this to avoid wounding their consciences. I must admit that during those years, I had to learn to balance what was sometimes just griping Christians against those who truly had convictions about eating out on Sunday. Needless to say, it was a great relief to all when even the grudging Christians changed their minds and began going out to eat on the Lord's Day.

Paul established the principle in 1 Corinthians 8:12: "When you sin against your brothers in this way and wound their weak conscience, you sin against Christ." So if you cannot tell when you're offending a sincere brother or just a griper, it is more Christlike to live your life so as not to sin against anyone's conscience.

Questions for Personal Reflection

1. How might a nonbeliever misunderstand your freedom in Christ? What should you do if someone misunderstands your freedom?

2. In what ways is it easy to abuse your freedoms and justify violating God's principles?

Day 5: My Personal Worship
Read Romans 12:1–2

J. B. Phillips translated Romans 12:2, "Don't let the world around you squeeze you into its own mould." You hold the key to the final form your Christianity takes. You alone decide just how far you will conform to the world's image of the "real man," the "independent woman," the "power executive." Finding what image to conform to is easy for the believer. Hang a picture of Jesus in the mental gallery of your life and do all you can at each waking moment to look like that picture.

There is a fable of a particular Persian prince who was born a hunchback. As he got older the prince realized that one day he would be the one who ruled the realm. His twisted form would not command the respect from his people he would have liked. In fact, it did not even demand his own respect. So as he advanced toward adolescence, he had the royal sculptor carve a stone statue of himself just as he would look when he became a grown man—if he were not hunchbacked. Soon the statue was finished and set in the courtyard just off his bedroom.

Then every day after the statue was in place, the Prince performed a strange ritual. He would go to the statue, remove his shirt from his deformed back, and stand back to back with his perfect alter ego. Then he would strain in what seemed a comical mode to throw his own twisted shoulders against the stately shoulder of the marble statue. At first people laughed at his comical ritual. But year by year—day by day—it seemed to all the world that the prince's back became straighter and straighter. Then one day, just before his coronation, he backed up to his statue and felt the thrilling touch of its cold marble shoulders against his own. He had become what he had striven to become.

Our own personal worship is meant to make us like Jesus. He is the great marble Christ whose image we should bear. Jesus is our statue, and our calling in worship is to become like him alone. No other standard will suffice.

Questions for Personal Reflection

1. What are you striving to become?

2. How does your goal compare to God's goal of conforming you to the image of Jesus Christ?

Day 6: Moses—Self-Control, the Key to God's Blessing

Read Exodus 15:22–27; Numbers 20:6–13

These are two easily contrasted passages that demonstrate the blessing that comes to us when we practice self-control. The two incidents are remarkably alike in some ways. In both instances the people are grumbling. In both instances hundreds of thousands of people are suffering from the heat and thirst. In both instances the people are critical. But notice the very different way that Moses responded in each of the circumstances.

First, in Exodus 15:22–27, there was water, but it was too bitter to drink. Moses cried out to the Lord, and the Lord showed him a piece of wood that he could throw into the bitter waters. Moses did this and the waters became sweet. Moses obeyed the Lord with perfect self-control and displayed no anger. The Lord said, "If you listen carefully to the voice of the LORD your God and do what is right in his eyes, if you pay attention to his commands and keep all his decrees, I will not bring on you any of the diseases I brought on the Egyptians, for I am the LORD, who heals you" (v. 26).

In the second instance, Moses became infuriated and lost his temper. God had said to him, "Speak to that rock before their eyes and it will pour out its water (Numbers 20:8). Unfortunately, "Moses took the staff from the LORD's presence, just as he commanded him. He and Aaron gathered the assembly together in front of the rock and Moses said to them, 'Listen, you rebels, must we bring you water out of this rock?'"

(vv. 9–10). Then in a fit of temper, he struck the rock and water gushed out. Everyone in Israel slaked their thirsts, but God said to Moses, because of his loss of control, "you will not bring this community into the land I give them" (v. 12). In a moment of lost self-control, Moses—who led the Israelites for forty years—was destined to never know for himself the joy of the Promised Land.

Still we must remember that except for that one notable loss of self-control, Moses was a man whose dynamic discipline produced a quality of leadership rarely known in this world. So glorious was this man of faith that the writer of Hebrews wrote of him: "By faith Moses, when he had grown up, refused to be known as the son of Pharaoh's daughter. He chose to be mistreated along with the people of God rather than to enjoy the pleasures of sin for a short time" (Hebrews 11:24–25). This statement alone speaks to Moses the man of self-denial, whose self-control was the key to all God's blessings.

Self-control feeds the soul, and the soul lives forever. Indulgence feeds the body—indeed it can overfeed the body—until its years are shortened, its health is gone, and it weeps that it lived for years but gleaned only a few minutes for God.

God enables the person of self-control to influence the world. The person who cannot or will not stand up to their own permissiveness is soon controlled by such massive addictions they are of no use to anyone. To say yes to all temptations is to become a slave to our indulgences, and to live for the microscopic reason of serving ourselves.

Questions for Personal Reflection

1. What keeps you from being concerned about feeding your soul?

2. What are some scriptures you can use to help you fend off any tendencies

toward self-indulgence?

Day 7: Group Discussion

The following questions should take about forty-five minutes to answer and discuss. Each member should answer the first question, leaving the remaining questions open-ended. Everyone need not answer, but be sure all members participate.

1. *What are our pet peeve sins, and what are the personal sins we tend to ignore?*

2. *How do your habits and hang-ups interfere with your ability to live out God's purpose for your life?*

3.   *Experiencing the fullness of God requires obedience to him. Why are people resistant to the idea of living in obedience to God?*

4.   *What are some of the ways in which your freedoms in Christ might be misunderstood by others?*

5.   *What are some of the images to which we try to conform our lives? What is the end result of these efforts?*

6.   *How can we make feeding our souls more important than feeding our bodies?*

Week 3: Self-Control—Saying No to Our Appetites

Memory Passage for the Week: 1 Corinthians 10:31

Day 1: Self-Control—Saying No to Our Appetites

To follow Christ is to say no to our appetites, take up our cross, and follow him. Exodus 32:19–26.

Day 2: The Purpose of God in My Life

Amos prophesied that a time was coming of siege and military destruction, when the indulgent would surrender their decadence in chains. Amos 4:1–2.

Day 3: My Relationship with Christ

Self-control must be in place to attain holiness, and holiness is the only foundation for a great relationship with Christ. Galatians 5:16, 19–21.

Day 4: My Service to Others

We make our lives effective by saying no to our appetites. We become spiritually effective as we practice self-control. 1 Corinthians 6:12–13.

Day 5: My Personal Worship

If we practice lives of temperance and faith, we will draw near to God. In his presence, our personal worship then becomes glorious. Leviticus 11:44.

Day 6: A Character Study on Paul

2 Corinthians 11:16–29

Day 7: Group Discussion

Day 1: Self-Control—Saying No to Our Appetites
Read Exodus 32:19–26

Idols. They require so little and give us so much of what we think we want to be in life. Idols are tangible; they are also visible. We can see a golden calf, touch a golden calf. Unlike the invisible, true God they can be comprehended by all the senses. In a word, idols are sensual.

When Moses came down from the mountain, he saw that Aaron, God's high priest, had become the high priest of Baal. When Moses asked him why he committed this atrocity, Aaron responded, "You know how prone these people are to evil. They said to me, 'Make us gods who will go before us. As for this fellow Moses who brought us up out of Egypt, we don't know what has happened to him.'... They gave me the gold, and I threw it into the fire, and out came this calf!'"(Exodus 32:22–24).

Aaron's deportment was self-excusing. He made it sound as though the calf made itself. "All I did," said Aaron, in essence, "was throw the gold into the fire and presto ... out came this false god. So, there you have it, Moses, I didn't have that much to do with it. The thing practically made itself!"

But Moses made no such excuse before the Lord. Moses took sin very seriously, saying, "You have committed a great sin. But now I will go up to the LORD; perhaps I can make atonement for your sin" (v. 30).

God, the Father of our Lord Jesus Christ, has always taught that the meaning of our lives lies in the things we deny ourselves. The doctrine of the golden calf teaches that meaning lies in our indulgence. If everyone were to obey every demand of every appetite, the world would be left in the charge of gluttons, rapists, murderers, and warlords. To follow Christ is to say no to our appetites, take up our cross, and follow him.

Questions for Personal Reflection

1. How have you allowed other things to interfere with your commitment to God?

2. What are some indulgences you should deny so that you can be more focused on your relationship with God?

Day 2: The Purpose of God in My Life

Read Amos 4:1–2

God has always been the champion of the poor. The poor are not closer to God because of their poverty, but their poverty creates a need for God. Israel had a problem with affluence. The problem with affluence is that it blinds the indulgent to the pain and suffering of the poor. The women of Israel were partygoers, eating and drinking in a country where the poor were sold into slavery for the price of a pair of shoes (Amos 2:6). Amos castigated these indulgent rich people on several other counts:

1. They denied justice to the oppressed (Amos 2:7).
2. A father and his son slept with the same temple prostitutes (Amos 2:7).
3. They horded, plundered, and looted in their fortresses (Amos 3:10).
4. They built summer palaces adorned with ivory (Amos 3:15).
5. They crushed the needy and oppressed the poor (Amos 4:1).
6. They were a culture of drunkenness (Amos 4:1).
7. They gave little but bragged about their temple offerings (Amos 4:5).
8. They forced the poor into sharecrop status (Amos 5:11).
9. They took bribes in the courts (Amos 5:12).

10. They worshiped astrology and the star gods (Amos 5:26).

11. They were gluttons (Amos 6:4).

All these indulgences and cruelties were clearly the telltale signs of a culture in its last throes. How closely they parallel our own times.

The number one question is: How can we learn self-control in the indulgent culture that we have become? Yes, it is not easy. Yet we must, for if we do not our own time in history will be lost and God's purpose in our lives can come to no avail.

Questions for Personal Reflection

1. Review the list of accusations and evaluate your life in each area. What should you change about your life so these things aren't true about you?

2. If these indulgences and cruelties are signs of a troubled culture, how troubled is your community and your home?

Day 3: My Relationship with Christ
Read Galatians 5:16, 19–21

Paul offered a four-word antidote to indulging ourselves in our appetites. His message was not one of negativity. His message was a positive one—a proactive approach that each individual believer can initiate and complete, not a hunkering down in false piety before our ferocious temptations. Paul's prescription for self-control involves standing up to our temptation and saying loudly and clearly, "Be gone, for I have given he who lives inside me complete charge of my life."

What is this four-word recipe for success in a life of self-control? Live by the Spirit! When we live by the Spirit, said the apostle, we will not indulge ourselves in the never-ending clamor of all those appetites that beg our indulgence and can destroy our life and witness forever.

What are these horrible flings at indulgence? See Galatians 5:19–21. To read these at first may seem like we are reading sins so terrible that we ourselves could never be guilty of them. But do not believe it. It is nothing more than the grace of God that keeps us from these sins at any given moment. Remember that indulgence rarely jumps into great crimes on the first leap. The truth is that we move into great sin through baby steps of compromise. Consider this list:

1. Sexual immorality begins in simple office flirtations.
2. Impurity and debauchery start with pornography.

3.   Ambition begins with buttering up the boss.

4.   Drunkenness begins with one little drink.

It is the little bargains we strike with Satan and with our consciences by which we lose our usefulness to Christ. To compromise even in little ways is to fail to live by the Spirit.

Questions for Personal Reflection

1. In what ways have you compromised and lost your usefulness to Christ?

2. How can that usefulness be restored?

Day 4: My Service to Others
Read 1 Corinthians 6:12–13

The apostle Paul believed that Christians were under no coercion to be moral. In fact, we have such liberty in the Lord that we can be a Christian and be as immoral as we please. We can love Jesus and do anything we want to, but the wonderful thing is that a true relationship with Jesus can change all our desires. The questions we have to face with every moral decision are two:

First: Is what I am deciding to do beneficial? In other words, what are the long-term benefits or consequences of this particular moral act I am deciding upon? Self-control mandates that we take the long look at our every moral or immoral deed. In this way we use good, sound reason to make our choices.

Second: Is what I'm about to do just one little step toward surrendering my long-term liberty? I will never forget an alcoholic who bragged, as all alcoholics are prone to do, "Liquor? Oh, I can take it or leave it. I just stop off at a bar every night on the way home and have two small martinis. I am not an alcoholic, I can stop any time I want."

I challenged him to come straight home three nights in a row and prove to me, to God, and to his family that he could take it or leave it. He discovered, to his dismay, that he was truly chemically dependent. This could have been avoided if he had asked the second question.

Paul said, "I will not be mastered by anything" (1 Corinthians 6:12). When we are truly free of any appetite controlling our lives, then we can turn and freely minister to others. But if we try to serve Christ and any other single appetite, we risk having something beside Jesus become the lord of our lives, making us far less useful to Christ.

Questions for Personal Reflection

1. What are some things you want to do that you know are a direct result of your faith in God?

2. How can you guard against falling into a way of life that is self-destructive and spiritually weak?

Day 5: My Personal Worship
Read Leviticus 11:44

"Consecrate yourselves," said Moses (Leviticus 11:44). What he really meant was, "Say no to those appetites that God forbids in your life." The end result is that when we have actually done this, we will be able to come into his presence, and our adoration of him will be sweet. But what was God really trying to accomplish with these taboos of Leviticus? Was God trying to get the Israelites to live a killjoy life in which they would always be on the lookout for sin and never really enjoy a single day of positive living?

Of course not.

Every taboo that God asks us to honor is for our sake and the sake of the kingdom of God. Take the Ten Commandments: were they spoken to regiment and restrict our freedom? It is not their constriction that is so important. At the center of every "thou shalt not" is a glorious liberty, not coercion. What kind of world would we have if everybody went around lying, stealing, murdering, and committing adultery at will? It is only because we honor these constrictions that we become truly free, and the world along with us.

The result of our honoring of God's commandments is true freedom. We have been set free by our own desire for holiness and in the practice of self-control. By entering into God's holiness, our worship is glorious.

Great worship sets us free from ourselves just as self-control makes sure that we stay in charge of our lives.

Questions for Personal Reflection

1. What are the benefits of the Ten Commandments in your life?

2. How can your obedience to God's commandments give you personal freedom?

Day 6: Paul—Self-Control, A Foundation of the Christian Faith
Read 2 Corinthians 11:16–29

The apostle Paul enumerated his hardships, blow by blow, only once in the Bible. Here he listed all that he experienced so that the name of Christ could be established in the world. To any who think that they have denied themselves excessively, the apostle would say:

> *I have worked much harder, been in prison more frequently, been flogged more severely, and been exposed to death again and again. Five times I received from the Jews forty lashes minus one. Three times I was beaten with rods, once I was stoned, three times I was shipwrecked, I spent a night and a day in the open sea. I have been constantly on the move. I have been in danger from rivers, in danger from bandits, in danger from my own countrymen, in danger from Gentiles; in danger in the city, in danger in the country, in danger at sea; and in danger from false brothers. I have labored and toiled and have often gone without sleep; I have known hunger and thirst and have often gone without food; I have been cold and naked. Besides everything else, I face daily the pressure of my concern for all the churches.*
> —2 Corinthians 11:23–28

Paul's hardships were summed up for the apostle under a single and simple rule: "I have been crucified with Christ and I no longer live, but Christ lives in me. The life I live in the body, I live by faith in the Son of God, who loved me and gave himself for me" (Galatians 2:20). Self-control and self-crucifixion were the same thing to the apostle. If he could put his ego on the cross, his selfish desires were all the easier to manage. Paul believed that self-control was just a part of the wonderful new life that he had been given to enjoy in Christ.

Paul knew our management of life is in direct relationship to our management of ourselves. This was true in a spiritual sense as well. Just as Christ gained mastery over death by dying, we, too, can gain mastery over all the world of temptation and sin by dying to ourselves.

> *In the same way, count yourselves dead to sin but alive to God in Christ Jesus. Therefore do not let sin reign in your mortal body so that you obey its evil desires. Do not offer the parts of your body to sin, as instruments of wickedness, but rather offer yourselves to God, as those who have been brought from death to life; and offer the parts of your body to him as instruments of righteousness. For sin shall not be your master, because you are not under law, but under grace.*
> —Romans 6:11–14

Self-control is dying to sin. But self-control is so much more than that: it is a kind of endurance, the kind of endurance that the apostle lived through so that the kingdom of God might become a reality in the world. All that Paul enumerated in 2 Corinthians 11—all that he suffered—he endured for the disciplines of self-control. This strong en-durance, this powerful self-control, enabled him to write almost half the New Testament and plant the gospel in Europe.

To control the self is to offer Christ a soul free of any other master. To control the self is to stand beyond the easy life and offer God the studied life. It is to say no to our appetites because we have "meat to eat that the world knows not of" (John 4:32). It is to pour out the wine of our addic-tions, because the water of life is better nectar.

Questions for Personal Reflection

1. How is your life one of endurance? What are the spiritual challenges you face on a regular basis?

2. How has your endurance produced spiritual strength? Where would you be right now if you lacked the power to overcome self-indulgence?

Day 7: Group Discussion

The following questions should take about forty-five minutes to answer and discuss. Each member should answer the first question, leaving the remaining questions open-ended. Everyone need not answer, but be sure all members participate.

1. *What are the "golden calves" we have created and now worship in our lives?*

2. *Are we more likely to address the needs of others or to ignore their needs? Explain your response.*

3. *Is your life producing the fruit of the Spirit or the fruit of indulgence? What changes do we need to make to produce the fruit of the Spirit?*

4. *How does faith in God affect the things we want to do? Is your list of things different from the lists of those who do not know Christ? If so, how? If not, why?*

5.   *What does it mean to live in the abundant life, and how do we achieve it?*

6.   *What are some things we can do to place our egos on the cross of Christ? Why is it important that we do this?*

Week 4: Self-Control—Managing Our Moods

Memory Passage for the Week: Psalm 42:5

Day 1: Self-Control—Managing Our Moods

Self-control speaks of getting a true view of self. The word itself does not encourage us to hate ourselves. It encourages us to take a long, hard look at who we are. 1 Samuel 19:8–17.

Day 2: The Purpose of God in My Life

When we lose control and fail to manage our moods, it is not just we who look bad; God's reputation is also damaged. Numbers 20:9–11.

Day 3: My Relationship with Christ

James and John wanted to call down fire on those who would not readily welcome Jesus into their village. They had missed the point. Luke 9:51–56.

Day 4: My Service to Others

The failure to manage our moods may scar the reputation of even the most noble. Acts 15:36–41.

Day 5: My Personal Worship

Believers are called to live lives of self-denial in times of cultural decadence. When we do, we can rejoice in defeating our own pride. Obadiah 2–4.

Day 6: A Character Study on John

John 1:19–34

Day 7: Group Discussion

Day 1: Self-Control—Managing Our Moods

Read 1 Samuel 19:8–17

The apostle Paul subjected each temptation to three tests. First, is it helpful? Second, is it constructive? Third, does it glorify God? (1 Corinthians 10:23, 31).

In the case of King Saul, an evil spirit occupied him, and when it did, all that Saul did was devious. He was clearly out of control. It seems he surrendered to evil and failed to face his temptations with these three questions.

The Greek word *egkratein* for "self-control" (otherwise translated "temperance") has to do with disciplining the self. Plato used the word for self-mastery. Paul used the word in 1 Corinthians 7:9 when he spoke of the Christians' mastery of sexual temptation. He used the word in 1 Corinthians 9:25 to speak of an athlete's disciplining of his body.

It is a word that speaks of getting the true view of the self. The word does not encourage us to hate ourselves. It encourages us to take a long, hard look at who we are. We are to be moderate as we understand and relate to our world.

As Martin Luther wrote, "We are at once saint and sinner." Self-control means that we make a conscious effort to make our saintliness more saintly and sinfulness less sinful. King Saul failed to make this effort; and the evil he wouldn't control, he ultimately couldn't control.

Questions for Personal Reflection

1. In what ways is your ego attempting to wrestle control of your life away from

God?

2. How can we maintain an accurate view of ourselves?

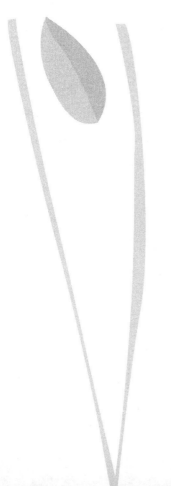

Day 2: The Purpose of God in My Life

Read Numbers 20:9–11

Moses lost his cool at the rock. It's not difficult to see that he could have made a pretty good case for why he behaved the way he did:

1. The people were always complaining—one of the perennial downers of leadership.

2. It was taking an extremely long time to conquer Canaan (it ultimately took forty years).

3. He didn't get much support from other team leaders, like Aaron, who tended to make golden calves when he stayed too long on Sinai.

4. Korah stirred up a popular rebellion against Moses' leadership.

5. The spies said Moses' objectives were unrealistic and the whole process should be abandoned.

6. His sister publicly opposed his leadership.

The Exodus in this passage appears to be a flop. With all of this baggage, to most of us, Moses losing his cool was nearly justifiable.

But God told him that the failure to manage his moods didn't just make him look foolish; it diminished the leadership of God.

When national evangelists become indulgent, people just quit supporting them, then turn away from God. When our failures keep us from acting out God's purpose in our lives, the implications can reach far wider than we might expect.

Questions for Personal Reflection

1. How do you respond when you see someone inaccurately reflect God's character?

2. What are some things you can do to keep from misrepresenting God?

Day 3: My Relationship with Christ
Read Luke 9:51–56

James and John wanted to call down fire on those who would not readily welcome Jesus into their village. James and John missed the point. You don't accept Christ and kill all unbelievers. Rather, you live like Christ and die for unbelievers.

Have you ever known Christians who seemed eager to torch the unbelieving world for the sake of good doctrine? I always wonder what would have happened if Jesus had replied to James and John, "Good idea, let's torch everybody who won't accept our doctrine." So James and John would have gone all through life scorching villages, and smiling while they burned.

Most people who get hostile with the gospel are really trying to help out—as they see it. But the controls they should invoke are not on the errant world but on their own errant selves. They shouldn't try to coerce the unbelieving world with thunderbolts. They should try to manage themselves, and once they have made self-control a working principle in their own lives, maybe the Samaritans might warm up to their propositions. Burning villages has never been a good evangelistic technique. On the other hand, burning our egos—our right to control others—has had an amazing effect.

Questions for Personal Reflection

1. Are you more likely to burn unbelievers or to burn your ego? Which is more beneficial to everyone?

2. What happens to relationships when we allow the gospel to become hostile?

Day 4: My Service to Others

Read Acts 15:36–41

The conflict at the end of Acts 15 might have been more of a personal crisis than traditionally imagined. Paul and Barnabas actually parted company over John Mark, whom Paul felt was a quitter and not dependable when hard times came. Barnabas disagreed, feeling that John Mark had matured since his earlier defection, and deserved a second chance. In the last letter Paul ever wrote, he seemed to have changed his mind about Mark (2 Timothy 4:11). We don't know exactly when he changed his mind; we only know that he did.

Managing our moods and getting our feelings about our viewpoints under control is so important in our service to others. I have come to believe there is only one real handicap that keeps us from serving others—our undisciplined lives. The major handicap to our evangelism is our own frail discipleship. Take the following people, for example, who made major impacts in spite of major obstacles:

Walter Scott was a cripple.

Dostoyevsky was epileptic.

Lincoln grew up in utter poverty.

Roosevelt was paralyzed.

Beethoven was deaf.

Helen Keller was blind and deaf.

Yet all of these people astounded the world with achievements that required intense personal discipline.

The truly handicapped are those whose moods are uncontrollable. Those who try to serve Christ without disciplining their lives end up making their faith a kind of religious romance that they indulge themselves in every week or so. But those who can control their moods and manage their tempers keep the kingdom of God a believable, desirable place to seek.

Questions for Personal Reflection

1. How do your uncontrolled moods handicap your spiritual life? What can you do to keep this from happening?

2. Are you making it possible for people to serve God, or are you an obstacle because of your moods? What should you do if you discover you are a source of trouble?

Day 5: My Personal Worship
Read Obadiah 2–4

Self-control is less prone to be a factor in a culture that feels safe and impregnable. So it was with Edom. The Edomites—among the nations east of Jordan—were the desert's only superpower. There was no one who could bring them down, or so they thought. But, in the end, they were brought down never to rise again. How often foolish pride precedes a fall! Think of all the indulgent boasts that come to nothing. The Spanish Armada could not be beaten. The Maginot line could not be crossed. The Berlin Wall would stand forever. The Hindenburg was the safest way to cross the ocean. Consider the foolishness of *ne plus ultra,* the idea that nothing existed beyond the Pillars of Hercules. Hitler's bunker was impregnable. They said the *Titanic* was unsinkable. Communism would dominate the twentieth century, Germany would never rise from the ashes of World War I, and the Vietnam War would be cleaned up in six months with U.S. involvement.

Pride! Pride! Pride!

How it always lures us into certain defeat. Of the twenty-eight civilizations that have occupied the center stage of world history, not one of them was crushed from the outside until they first had decayed and rotted from the inside.

Self-control is rarely a virtue of the proud. Security breeds indulgence and death—national death. Still, we believers are called to live lives of self-denial in times of cultural decadence. Then shall we triumph over that small pitiable pride that defeated Edom.

Questions for Personal Reflection

1. Pride is the opposite of self-control. Is your life characterized more by pride or by self-control? Explain your response.

2. How can you maintain your dependence on God while experiencing spiritual growth and victory?

Day 6: John—Who We Are in Relationship to Christ

Read John 1:19–34

John the Baptist's self-control took the form of rigorous self-denial. He lived in the wilderness when he could have lived in town. He ate locusts and wild honey when he could have had a more normal diet. He dressed in animal skins in an era when tunics and togas were common. Why? Because he understood who he was and what God had called him to do.

But the godliest form of his self-control came when he defined himself to the mob. They asked him who he was, and at any one of their questioning points he might have lied about who he was and taken the glory that belonged to Christ alone. But when they asked him their famous "Are you?" questions, he answered out of integrity. He gave them honest answers. He might have lied about who he was and taken the esteem he would offer none but Jesus. We must remember that at this time in his ministry, John was better known and more popular than the Christ he came to introduce. Catch this dialogue (John 1:21–23):

> *"Are you Elijah?"*
> *He said, "I am not."*
> *"Are you the Prophet?"*
> *He answered, "No."*
> *Finally they said, "Who are you? Give us an answer to take back to those who sent us. What do you say about yourself?"*

> *John replied in the words of Isaiah the prophet, "I am the*
> *voice of one calling in the desert, 'Make straight the way for*
> *the Lord.'"*

At any of these places John might have acted to build his own reputation, but always he answered truthfully, "I am not the Christ" (v. 20).

His most glorious metaphor of identity compared him to a trumpet playing a fanfare for the approach of a king. When you hear the fanfare, you do not ask for the name of the man who plays the trumpet, you ask the name of the approaching king. John the Baptist was a trumpet in the wilderness.

In all of this he practiced self-control, and in every act of self-identification, John said very clearly that Jesus was the big deal, not him. John told us all that self-control is remembering who we are in relationship to Christ.

Self-control is the result of self-denial. Self-denial is the practice of seeing our lives in terms of other people. We were not put on this earth to be the gluttons of God's abundance. We were put here to reclaim the world by trading joy in lesser things for a kind of joyous abundance that we only find by denying ourselves. With the words "I renounce," God gives us a trumpet to announce the King.

Questions for Personal Reflection

1. In what ways is your life serving to benefit other people?

2. How should you respond when you are tempted to identify yourself as anyone other than a servant of Jesus Christ?

Day 7: Group Discussion

The following questions should take about forty-five minutes to answer and discuss. Each member should answer the first question, leaving the remaining questions open-ended. Everyone need not answer, but be sure all members participate.

1.   *What areas of life do you find it most difficult to be disciplined?*

2.   *What are the dangers of losing control of our moods? Which moods are often the most overwhelming or destructive?*

3.   *How are you developing relationships that will ultimately provide you the opportunity to share your faith? Why are these types of relationships important?*

4.   *How do you keep your spiritual life from becoming undisciplined?*

5. *How can we keep from rotting spiritually?*

6. *What can we do to keep from taking credit for the work Christ does through us?*

Week 5: Self-Control—The Disciplined Life

Memory Passage for the Week: Ephesians 4:1

Day 1: Self-Control—The Disciplined Life

Discipline is a synonym for self-control. 1 Corinthians 9:24–27.

Day 2: The Purpose of God in My Life

Simply to be disciplined for discipline's sake is not God's purpose for our lives. But to practice discipline allows us to become effective ministers to others. Proverbs 1:1–6.

Day 3: My Relationship with Christ

Every heartbeat brings us closer to the finale. Jesus is coming. It ought to make us more disciplined and more serious about productive living. 1 Peter 4:7.

Day 4: My Service to Others

We should work hard to use and improve on the gifts God gives us as his Spirit enters us. Then our lives will be always under renovation and the church will be furnished for her work in the world. 1 Timothy 4:13–16.

Day 5: My Personal Worship

The disciplined life always ends in victory. 2 Timothy 4:6–8.

Day 6: The Parable of the Ten Bridesmaids

Matthew 25:1–13 (TLB)

Day 7: Group Discussion

Day 1: Self-Control—The Disciplined Life

Read 1 Corinthians 9:24–27

When I think of the movie Chariots of Fire, I can't help but think of athletes charging down the cinder lanes, legs driving like pistons, arms pumping like jackhammers, the lungs gasping for enough oxygen to finish the race. What a strong image of discipline this is.

Discipline is a synonym for self-control.

Paul reminded the Corinthians that they were to run, and run, and run. Run, said the apostle, in such a way as to get the prize. But this is more than a mere athletic contest. Athletes are in the business of gold medals. An athlete's effective, competitive years are seldom more than ten. Then if he or she has not won the medal, others who are just leaving adolescence will be banging at the doors of their success, ready to claim their prize.

But Paul had noticed that as he got older the areas of Christian discipline had become even harder for him. He testified that he had "to beat his body" (1 Corinthians 9:27) to contain and keep up the rigors of Christian discipline.

"Beat his body"? What could he mean? Just this: As we get older, we find the old bones are heavier with past achievements. The old muscles are weaker from years of service. When the alarm goes off, it is easier to slap the "snooze" button and let ourselves sleep a little longer. So we have to "beat" our weak intentions to try and make ourselves as spiritually productive as when we were younger.

So Paul said he intended to be self-controlled, disciplined—"lest after he had preached to others, he himself should be a castaway" (1 Corinthians 9:27 KJV).

Questions for Personal Reflection

1. What are some things you do to maintain your spiritual productivity?

2. Paul realized that spiritual discipline was tough. Do you agree with Paul? Why or why not?

Day 2: The Purpose of God in My Life
Read Proverbs 1:1–6

Self-control is the opening theme of the book of Proverbs. The writer said that self-control makes those who honor it effective in these four areas:

1. **Wisdom** is not intelligence. Wisdom is that God-given ability to use our intelligence.

2. **Discipline** is the ability to do the things that are good for us, rather than opting for those things that are fun or easy for us. Jesus' wilderness temptations were all Satan's easy options for proving Jesus was the Messiah without the ugly necessity of the Cross. But Jesus was not bought off.

3. **Understanding** is that gift of God that sits and waits, and then sorts and sifts through all the information available before it makes a decision on anything. Understanding is insight that floods the dark heart with light, but only after it has done its homework.

4. **Doing what is right and fair:** Most of us have no problem doing what is right once we have determined what right is. We ought always to pray that the Lord gives us the power to do the right thing, as we can be sure of what it is.

Our ministry to others is always God's big purpose in our lives. This passage in Proverbs says that there are three areas of self-control as we minister to others:

1. We are to give prudence to the simple. Simply put, giving prudence to the simple means that we have a ministry of helping others think things through.

2. We are to furnish discretion to the young. "Brash" is often a more common adjective to describe the young than "discreet." Yet the young often need a little cross-generational insight to help them handle life.

3. We are to give guidance to those who lack insight. The understanding of deeper truths can only be supplied by more mature teachers to less mature students.

Questions for Personal Reflection

1. How are you involved in the ministry of helping others?

2. What are some of your excuses for those times when you have failed to help others?

Day 3: My Relationship with Christ

Read 1 Peter 4:7

"The end of all things is near" (1 Peter 4:7). The world is in rehearsal for the grand event. Time is always "on the brink." Every culture has been possessed of strong millennial movements.

The Cromwellian government in England knew the fiery Adventism of the Fifth Monarchists, who believed the monarchy of Charles I was precedent to the coming of Christ.

In 1844 the Millerites assembled in white to await the Second Coming.

In the latter part of the nineteenth century, the Amana colonists moved from Germany to Iowa because their Adventism was unwelcome in the old country.

The Jehovah's Witnesses have always believed that Jesus is coming soon, and they have set various dates for the event.

The rise of Hitler led American evangelists to believe he was the Antichrist and Jesus would soon be coming again.

The Cuban Missile Crisis had evangelical preachers everywhere preaching the close proximity of the Second Coming.

The Late Great Planet Earth by Hal Lindsey explained how the European Common Market was evidence of the nearness of the Second Coming. It still remains one of evangelicalism's best-selling books.

More recently we were daily besieged with much Y2K talk related to the Second Coming.

Peter, like these other theorists, reminded us that time is short, and though no one knows the exact time or date when Jesus will return, his message should prompt us to self-control and holy living. Peter said it even so well in his second letter:

> *Since everything will be destroyed in this way, what kind of people ought you to be? You ought to live holy and godly lives as you look forward to the day of God and speed its coming.*
>
> —2 Peter 3:11–12

The calendar is dying. The sand is all but through the hourglass. Now is the time to take charge of our lives.

Questions for Personal Reflection

1. How often do you think about the fact that any day could be the day that Christ returns? How should this reality affect your daily life?

2. Why do we often attempt to excuse our disobedience by placing blame on someone else? What effect does blame have on personal responsibility?

Day 4: My Service to Others

Read 1 Timothy 4:13–16

Paul, the elder, recommended to Timothy, the younger, a fourfold course of discipline for preachers:

1. Public reading of the Scripture
2. Preaching
3. Teaching
4. Developing the special gift

Not all of us are called to be preachers, but this "special gift" is to be the key focus of our disciplines. Paul said was given special gifts at the laying on of hands. We all want to appreciate those genetic gifts, or talents, that are given to us through DNA. These gifts made Caruso sing, Cassatt paint, and Hemingway write.

Timothy's special gift, however, was a gift of a different kind. It wasn't born in him. It didn't come through his DNA. It came to him when the elders laid their hands on him, and there on the spot God gave him a gift that God alone would use to advance his kingdom.

Then Timothy was then able to better serve because he took this beautiful thing God gave him and developed it to the point that he used it all for God's glory.

Paul names these spiritual gifts in three different passages: Romans 12, 1 Corinthians 12, and Ephesians 4. Gifts are given by God specifically to enlarge his church and make it more effective. These gifts are not given in the fullest state of their development. God gives them as diamonds in the rough. We spend the rest of our lives developing and improving those gifts and working them out (Philippians 2:12).

But God's mandate of self-control is that we never neglect improving the gift God gave us as his spirit entered us. Then our lives will be always under renovation and the church will be furnished for her work in the world.

Questions for Personal Reflection

1. How are you using your spiritual gifts in service to God?

2. What are some things you can do to develop your spiritual gifts?

Day 5: My Personal Worship

Read 2 Timothy 4:6–8

Personal discipline over a lifetime always wins the crown of life. But self-control is not the kind of discipline that hurries us from one holy agenda to the next. Sometimes those who are self-control–aholics are those who appear to be the most driven in holiness. The key is pacing. Those who pace their self-control live longer, and their longevity presents to God full, well paced years instead of hurried, neuroses-driven good deeds.

Pacing our lives, and consistency in our worship are matters of self-control. Paul arrived in heaven, having written half of the New Testament and starting dozens of churches over three missionary journeys. He didn't get to heaven as soon as he originally wished, but he took many people into gospel freedom with him.

Pacing in life should never bypass joy, and our worship should never be grudging. The joy of our discipline ought to possess us from day to day. Consistent, joyous worship is essential to a paced and disciplined life. When we fail to stop, slow down, and focus entirely on praising our Lord, we chase the holiness out of our hearts and out of our worship.

Questions for Personal Reflection

1. Is worship, for you, a time of slowing, centering, and focusing on God? Do you worship consistently? How can you develop this discipline in your life?

2. Does discipline bring you joy? Why or why not?

Day 6: The Parable of the Ten Bridesmaids

MATTHEW 25:1–13 (TLB)

The kingdom of Heaven can be illustrated by the story of ten brides-maids who took their lamps and went to meet the bridegroom. But only five of them were wise enough to fill their lamps with oil, while the other five were foolish and forgot.

So, when the bridegroom was delayed, they lay down to rest un-til midnight, when they were roused by a shout, "The bridegroom is coming! Come out and welcome him!"

All the girls jumped up and trimmed their lamps. Then the five who hadn't any oil begged the others to share with them, for their lamps were going out.

But the others replied, "We haven't enough. Go instead to the shops and buy some for yourselves."

But while they were gone, the bridegroom came, and those who were ready went in with him to the marriage feast, and the door was locked.

Later, when the other five returned, they stood outside, calling, "Sir, open the door for us!"

But he called back, "Go away! It is too late!"

So stay awake and be prepared, for you do not know the date or the moment of my return.

Questions for Personal Reflection

1. Are you ready for Christ's return? What has made you ready?

2. How are you helping make others ready for Christ's return?

Day 7: Group Discussion

The following questions should take about forty-five minutes to answer and discuss. Each member should answer the first question, leaving the remaining questions open-ended. Everyone need not answer, but be sure all members participate.

1. *Why are the spiritual disciplines so hard to pursue, obtain, and keep?*

2. *How can we obtain wisdom?*

3. *What are some ways to make wisdom come alive in our lives?*

4. *In light of the second coming of Christ, how should we live each day?*

5. *How can we discover our spiritual gifts, and what is their ultimate purpose?*

6. *What is the relationship between self-control and holiness? Which one comes first?*

Week 6: Self-Control—Freedom from Permissiveness

Memory Passage for the Week: Titus 1:7–8

Day 1: Self-Control—Freedom from Permissiveness

The person who remains temperate in one area will likely be temperate in other areas. 2 Kings 21:1–9.

Day 2: The Purpose of God in My Life

We serve a good Master who loves us to the point that he is willing to die for us. We are truly free, not to have our own way, but to do something meaningful in the world. Romans 6:22–23.

Day 3: My Relationship with Christ

Haggai wanted to set people free from their own permissiveness. To be happy by having more and more while giving less and less of ourselves to Christ is no better than a bucket with holes in it. Haggai 1:5–6.

Day 4: My Service to Others

A nation can only arrive at self-control when her individual citizens put it into practice. Joel 3:1–3.

Day 5: My Personal Worship

When God gets our best, and we give it freely, we have set ourselves free of the permissive and immoral life. Malachi 1:6–8.

Day 6: Verses for Further Reflection

Day 7: Group Discussion

Day 1: Self-Control—Freedom from Permissiveness
Read 2 Kings 21:1–9

There is one name that stands as the arch-villain in the lineage of all the kings of Judah. That name is Manasseh. Consider the nature of all the evil things he did:

- He built high places for star worship (2 Kings 21:3).
- He built temples of sacred prostitution to Baal and Asherah (2 Kings 21:3).
- He worshiped astral deities (2 Kings 21:3).
- He built idols in the very temple of God. When the Seleucids later offered a pig on the altar, Daniel referred to this sacrifice as the Abomination of Desolation (2 Kings 21:4–5; Daniel 11:31).
- He sacrificed his own son in the fiery arms of Molech (2 Kings 21:6).
- He practiced witchcraft and the evil arts (2 Kings 21:6).
- He went to séances (2 Kings 21:6).
- He lived a more wicked life than did the Amorites that Israel had conquered to establish the holiness of God in the land.

Manasseh was indulgent. Indulgence is a comfort-loving attitude that constantly makes a wider bed for itself. Indulgence and self-control are alike in one way: they are both addictive. For instance, a person who is sexually free will continue to push this latitude into wider and wider areas of permissiveness. Not just that, but indulgence in one area—like sexuality—is also easily extended to alcoholism or gluttony.

Across the gamut from indulgence lies self-control. When we deny any appetite, it is easier to extend that strength into other areas. The person who remains temperate in one area will likely be temperate in other areas.

What made Manasseh Judah's most evil king? He likely lacked the ability to say no to himself. He skirted self-denial, opting for the "if it feels good, do it" philosophy. He likely thought he was living free, but little did he know, he was enslaved by the ugliest of monsters—his own permissiveness!

Questions for Personal Reflection

1. How does the "if it feels good, do it" philosophy affect your life?

2. What is the role of Scripture in combating this philosophy?

Day 2: The Purpose of God in My Life

Read Romans 6:22–23

I rarely meet a person who is so free that their freedoms are destroying them. But here and there I meet a person like Harry. When Harry was in high school, he began to overeat. He loved food—all food—but particularly junk food. Harry loved life and good times and even though he claimed to be a Christian, Harry would confess, "Well, Jesus wants us to enjoy life." By the time Harry was out of high school he weighed 250 pounds—the next time I saw him in his mid-twenties, he weighed 400 pounds. His lack of self-control finally had pushed his indulgences to the max.

The last time I visited Harry he was living in a mobile home. I entered his home, struck by the incongruities of how Harry had gotten into the mobile home. I felt sure it could not have been the same narrow door I had used to enter his home. When I saw him, spread across the width of an entire sofa, I smiled and we conversed congenially, but as we engagingly spoke to each other he was eating a can of cherry pie filling directly from the can.

Was Harry free, free to eat anything he wanted? Of course not. Harry was enslaved.

Paul said that self-control is being set free of the sin of too much freedom. Then we voluntarily opt to place our indulgences directly in the hands of Christ. And as we surrender our old indulgent lifestyles, we are set free of our destructive freedoms and given charge of a glorious new freedom—obedience to the Lord of our self-control.

The moment we are saved, we are empowered, not to control the world but to control ourselves. When we are in charge of our own lives, we realize we have been given the greatest of all gifts—freedom from destructive permissiveness.

Questions for Personal Reflection

1. How can permissiveness be destructive in your life?

2. What are some ways you can control the abuse of permissiveness in your life?

Day 3: My Relationship with Christ
Read Haggai 1:5–6

Haggai wanted to set people free from their own permissiveness. He called them to remembrance that the temptation to do it if it feels good was an open-ended proposition. To be happy by having more while we give God less is a bucket with holes in it.

> *You have planted much, but have harvested little.*
> *You eat, but you never have enough.*
> *You put on clothes, but are not warm.*
> *You earn wages, only to put them in a purse with holes in it.*
> —Haggai 1:6

Indulgence is the key to happiness, or so we are told. The pitch of nearly all the ad-men is, go ahead and indulge.

"Let yourself go," entices one fast-food merchant.

"Pamper yourself," says another seller.

"Have it your way," says yet another.

"You deserve a break today," is most alluring. So is "Come fly away with us," or "Take the ride of your life."

Hardly any national advertising firms say, "Hey! Deny yourself! You must stop letting yourself go! You've pampered yourself far too long! You don't deserve a break today, so stop having it your way!"

Haggai reminded us that all the fun we think we're having by letting ourselves go can get out of hand. It's time to set ourselves free of these killing freedoms that destroy our lives bit by bit.

I had a friend who said he had conquered fundamentalist legalism and was free to take a drink whenever he wanted; sadly, he died an alcoholic.

I had a friend who said he was sexually faithful—generally—but he liked to window-shop; he eventually left his wife for another woman. His children have never recovered.

I had a friend who felt he could get around some tax laws, and he's now spent four years in prison.

Haggai said we can only develop a close relationship with God when we quit serving ourselves. Only then can we really convince God that we ourselves are not gods.

Questions for Personal Reflection

1. In what areas of life are you likely to let permissiveness get out of control?

2. Are you more inclined to serve yourself or to serve God? How do you keep from serving yourself?

Day 4: My Service to Others
Read Joel 3:1–3

Nations generally move from a patriotic, values-driven culture toward a culture of indulgence and moral decay. Joel said God wanted to reckon with the Israelites over the degeneration of the nation's morality. God basically said, "I am going to judge Israel for institutionalizing sin." The sin life of a nation grew from individual indulgences to the decay of national character.

How do we live in a culture where indulgence is the rule while we try to live out of a context of self-control? It is hard for Christian parents to say to their children, "You cannot go," only to hear their children say, "But Jennifer's parents let her." How do we teach values that derive from our self-control when the world is a "just do it" culture?

If we are going to minister to others, we must belong to Christ in such a way that pleasing him with our lifestyle means everything to us. When we minister to others, they will try to say to us, "I could never be a Christian because Christians don't ..."

Sin grows gradually from our wholehearted condemnation to wholesale acceptance. We are first horrified by sin, then only shocked, then we only argue about it. Later, we're conversational with it. Then we are congenial about it. Finally, at last, we are indulgent. My service to others means that I'm going to serve others, with a full understanding of the tendency we all have to opt for the easy way instead of self-control.

Questions for Personal Reflection

1. What are some things you do that are not beneficial to you or to the community? Why do you do these things?

2. How has sin slipped into your life and caught you off-guard? How can you keep that from happening again in the future?

Day 5: My Personal Worship
Read Malachi 1:6–8

The most certain sign that we have sold out to the indulgent life can be seen in the difference between what we give God and what we keep for ourselves.

> *Will a man rob God? Yet you rob me.*
> *But you ask, "How do we rob you?"*
> *In tithes and offerings. You are under a curse—the whole*
> *nation of you—because you are robbing me.*
> *Bring the whole tithe into the storehouse, that there may be*
> *food in my house. Test me in this ... and see if I will not throw*
> *open the floodgates of heaven and pour out so much blessing*
> *that you will not have room enough for it.*
> —Malachi 3:8–10

Robbing God? What were the Israelites doing with the money they stole from God? Well, they were using it to "feather their own nests." The money we give to God shows how much we love God. The money we withhold from God shows how much we love ourselves. So in most ways the more we refuse to give sacrificially to God, the more we exhibit our own self-indulgence.

It is better to tithe than to not tithe. Inevitably people argue, "Oh, I don't want to be so legalistic, so I don't tithe." But tithing wasn't God's idea so that he could take our little and have much. After all, he owns the world. What could our tithe add to his universal ownership? But God knows that what we hold on to is much more likely to spoil us than that which we give. If we keep all that we make for ourselves, we will not be the master of all we own, but instead a slave.

Questions for Personal Reflection

1. What does your giving record say about your relationship with God?

2. What are some of the reasons people don't give to God?

Day 6: Verses for Further Reflection

Matthew 4:9–11: "All this I will give you," he said, "if you will bow down and worship me." Jesus said to him, "Away from me, Satan! For it is written: "Worship the Lord your God, and serve him only." Then the devil left him, and angels came and attended him.

Luke 9:23: Then he said to them all: "If anyone would come after me, he must deny himself and take up his cross daily and follow me."

Mark 14:36: "Abba, Father," he said, "everything is possible for you. Take this cup from me. Yet not what I will, but what you will."

Matthew 19:17: "Why do you ask me about what is good?" Jesus replied. "There is only One who is good. If you want to enter life, obey the commandments."

1 Thessalonians 5:6, 8: So then, let us not be like others, who are asleep, but let us be alert and self-controlled.... But since we belong to the day, let us be self-controlled, putting on faith and love as a breastplate, and the hope of salvation as a helmet.

2 Timothy 1:7: For God did not give us a spirit of timidity, but a spirit of power, of love and of self-discipline.

Titus 2:11–12: For the grace of God that brings salvation has appeared to all men. It teaches us to say "No" to ungodliness and worldly passions, and to live self-controlled, upright and godly lives in this present age.

ROMANS 1:18–32

In this passage Paul showed the clear evidence of those who have lost all self-control. The indulgences of life lead to idolatries of one kind or another. The idolatries lead to hedonism. The choice in life is either self-control or moral irrelevance.

The wrath of God is being revealed from heaven against all the godlessness and wickedness of men who suppress the truth by their wickedness, since what may be known about God is plain to them, because God has made it plain to them. For since the creation of the world God's invisible qualities—his eternal power and divine nature—have been clearly seen, being understood from what has been made, so that men are without excuse.

For although they knew God, they neither glorified him as God nor gave thanks to him, but their thinking became futile and their foolish hearts were darkened. Although they claimed to be wise, they became fools and exchanged the glory of the immortal God for images made to look like mortal man and birds and animals and reptiles.

Therefore God gave them over in the sinful desires of their hearts to sexual impurity for the degrading of their bodies with one another. They exchanged the truth of God for a lie, and worshiped and served created things rather than the Creator—who is forever praised. Amen.

Because of this, God gave them over to shameful lusts. Even their women exchanged natural relations for unnatural ones. In the same way the men also abandoned natural relations with women and were inflamed with lust for one another. Men committed indecent acts with other men, and received in themselves the due penalty for their perversion.

Furthermore, since they did not think it worthwhile to retain the knowledge of God, he gave them over to a depraved mind, to do what ought not to be done. They have become filled with every kind of wickedness, evil, greed and depravity. They are full of envy, murder, strife, deceit and malice. They are gossips, slanderers, God-haters, insolent, arrogant and boastful; they invent ways of doing evil; they disobey their parents; they are senseless, faithless, heartless, ruthless. Although they know God's righteous decree that those who do such things deserve death, they not only continue to do these very things but also approve of those who practice them.

Questions for Personal Reflection

1. How can we keep the words of the above passage from being true about us?

2. How many of the things mentioned in this passage are accepted as normal today? What should be the believer's response to these things?

Day 7: Group Discussion

The following questions should take about forty-five minutes to answer and discuss. Each member should answer the first question, leaving the remaining questions open-ended. Everyone need not answer, but be sure all members participate.

1. *Indulgence and self-control are at opposite ends of the same spectrum. How can we keep our lives under control?*

2. *How can we keep God's agenda rather than pursuing our own agendas?*

3.   *What is the role of individuals in restoring moral decency in our land?*

4.   *What is the danger of giving God our second best?*

5.   *Why is it important to offer God our tithes and offerings?*

6.   *What are we saying to God when we refuse to give to him?*

PRAYER JOURNAL

Use the following pages to record both prayer requests and answers.